EASY PIANO

BEST OF
NORAH JONES

Cover photo © WENN Rights Ltd / Alamy Stock Photo

ISBN 978-1-70510-798-0

Visit Hal Leonard Online at
www.halleonard.com

Contact us:
Hal Leonard
7777 West Bluemound Road
Milwaukee, WI 53213
Email: info@halleonard.com

In Europe, contact:
Hal Leonard Europe Limited
42 Wigmore Street
Marylebone, London, W1U 2RN
Email: info@halleonardeurope.com

In Australia, contact:
Hal Leonard Australia Pty. Ltd.
4 Lentara Court
Cheltenham, Victoria, 3192 Australia
Email: info@halleonard.com.au

CARRY ON

Words and Music by
NORAH JONES

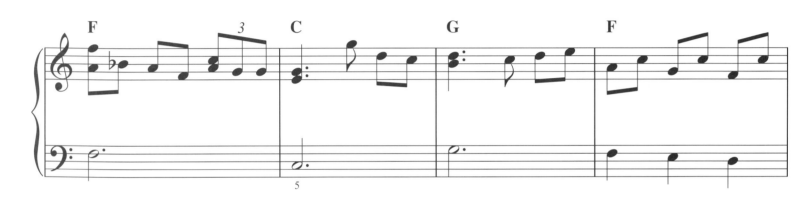

And af-ter all's _____ been said and done, _____ who said it best? _____
_____ the time to speak _____ and speak to me, _____

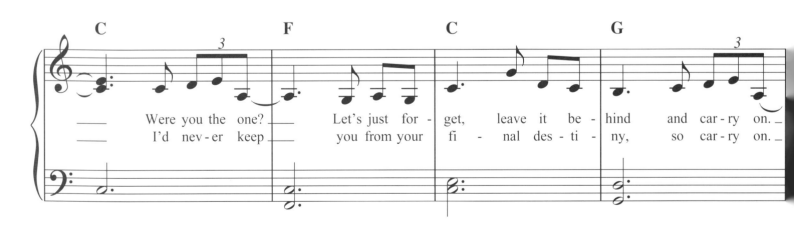

_____ Were you the one? _____ Let's just for-get, leave it be-hind and car-ry on.
_____ I'd nev-er keep _____ you from your fi-nal des-ti-ny, so car-ry on.

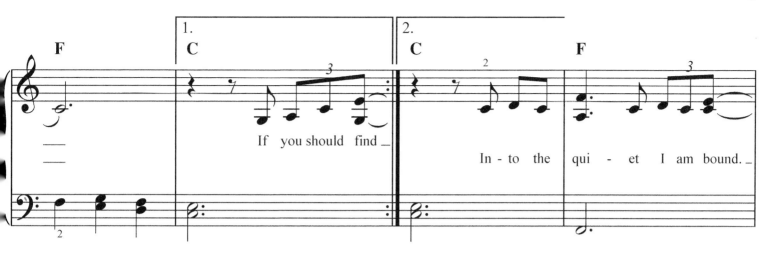

If you should find __

In - to the qui - et I am bound. __

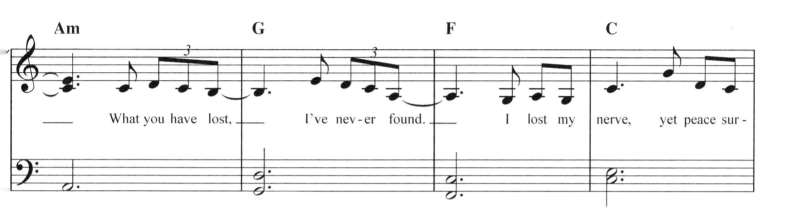

What you have lost, __ I've nev - er found. __ I lost my nerve, yet peace sur -

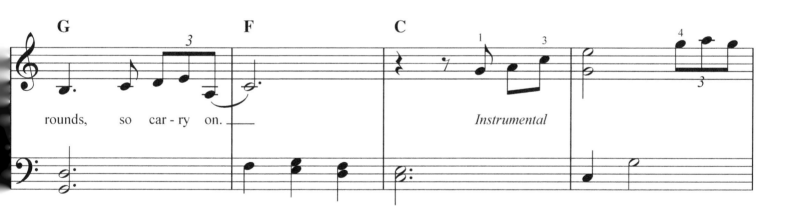

rounds, so car - ry on. __ *Instrumental*

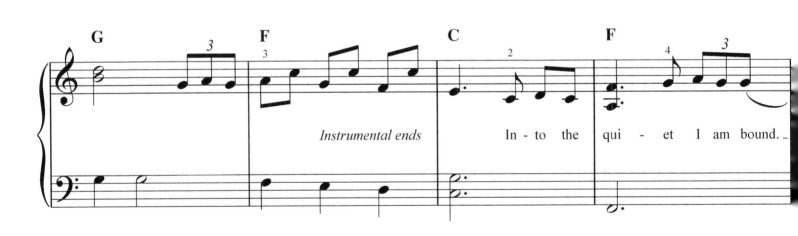

Instrumental ends   In - to the qui - et I am bound. __

__ What you have lost, __ I've nev - er found. __ I lost my nerve, yet peace sur -

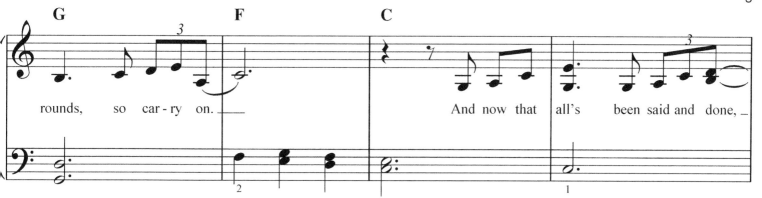

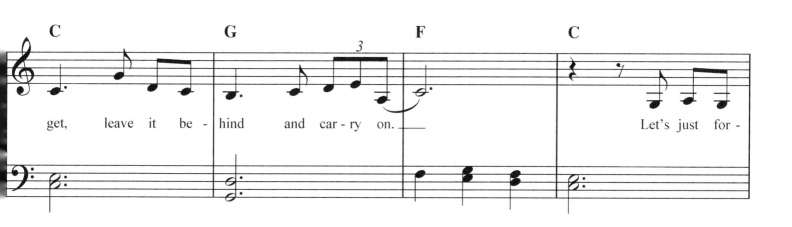

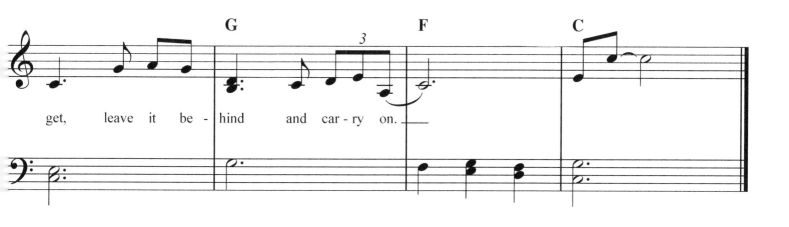

CHASING PIRATES

Words and Music by
NORAH JONES

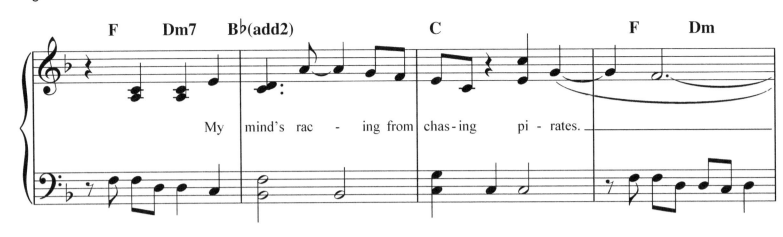

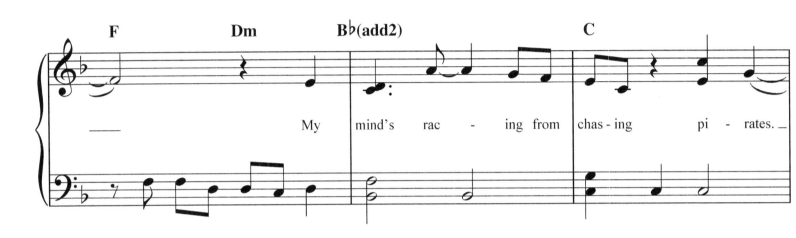

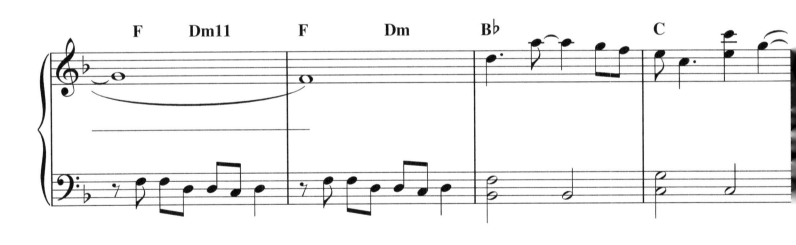

COME AWAY WITH ME

Words and Music by
NORAH JONES

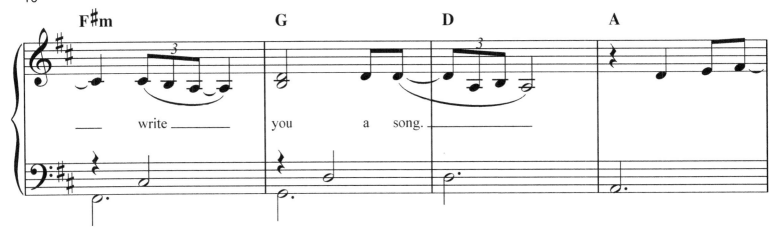

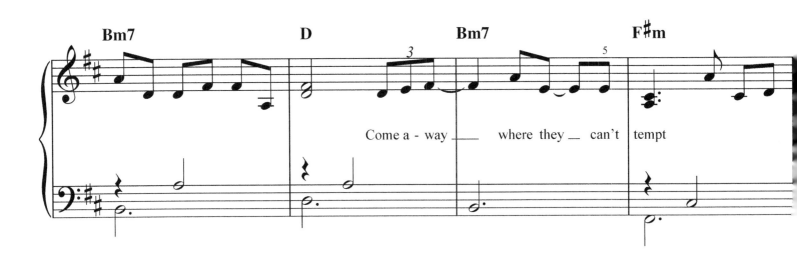

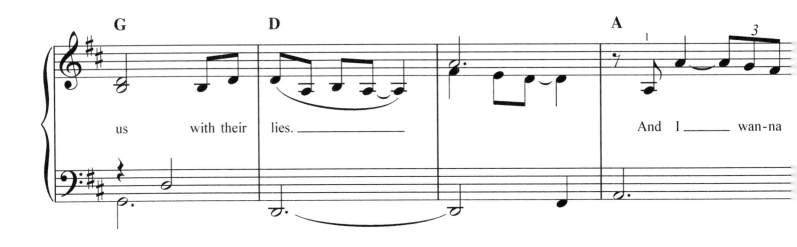

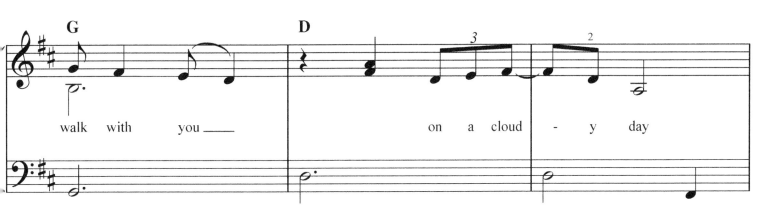

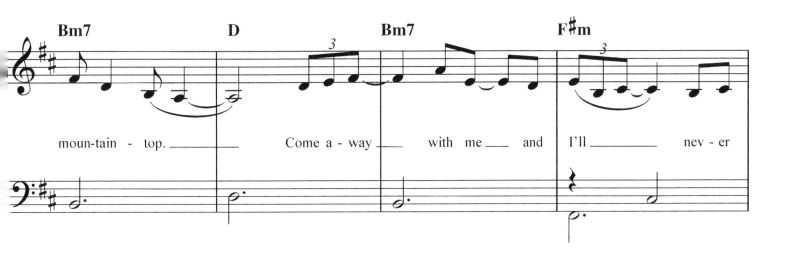

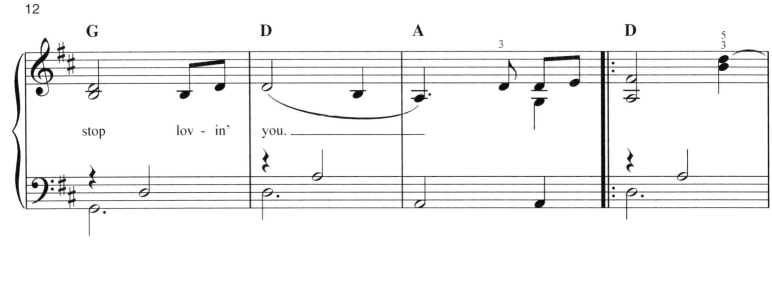

stop   lov - in'   you. _____

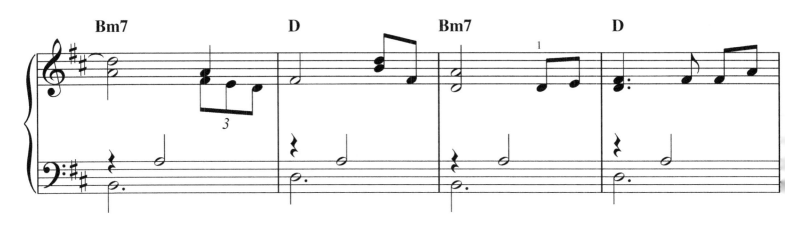

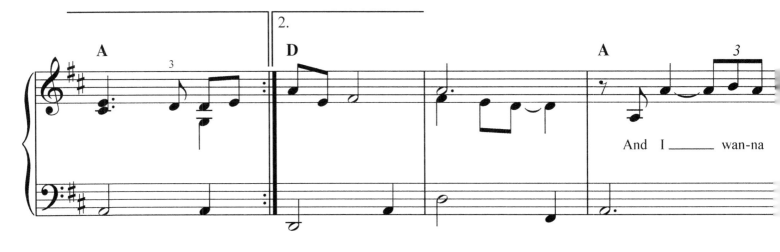

And I _____ wan-na

wake up ___ with the rain ___ fall - in' on a tin roof ___ while I'm

safe there ___ in your arms. So all I ___ ask is ___ for you to come a - way ___

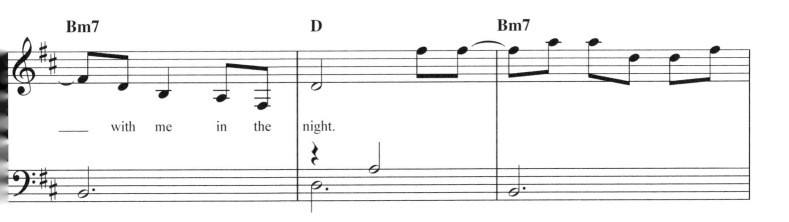

___ with me in the night.

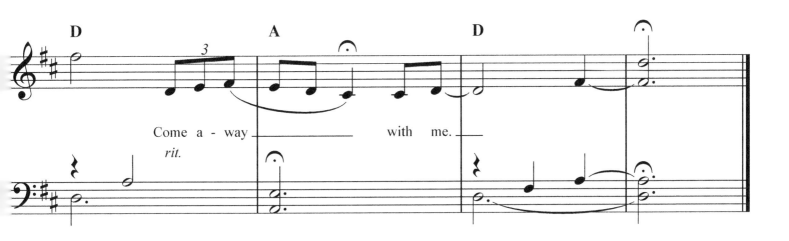

Come a - way ___ with me. ___

rit.

FLIPSIDE

Words and Music by NORAH JONES
and PETER REMM

Blues Rock

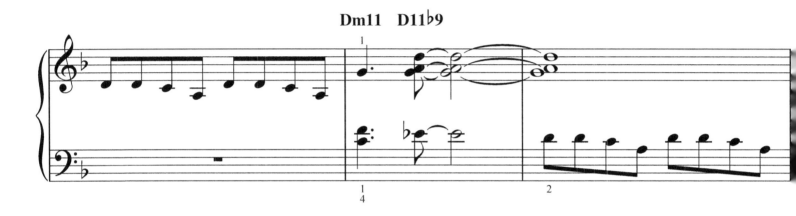

Dm7

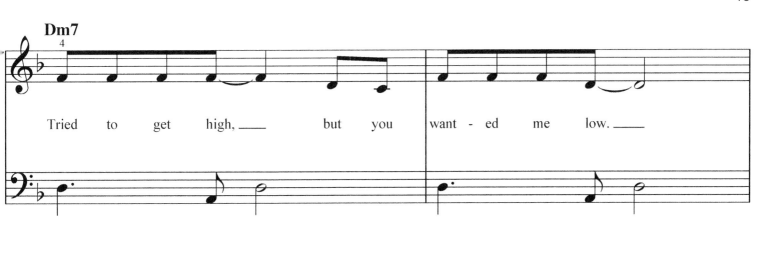

Tried to get high, ____ but you want - ed me low. ____

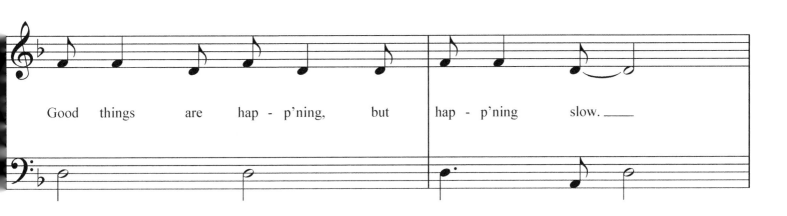

Good things are hap - p'ning, but hap - p'ning slow. ____

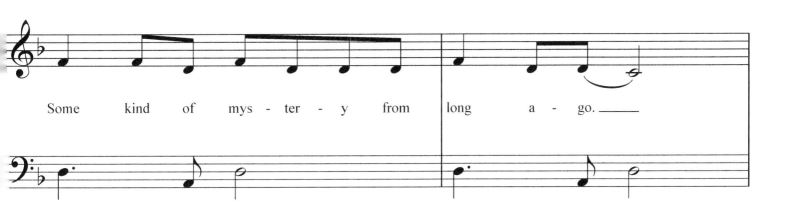

Some kind of mys - ter - y from long a - go. ____

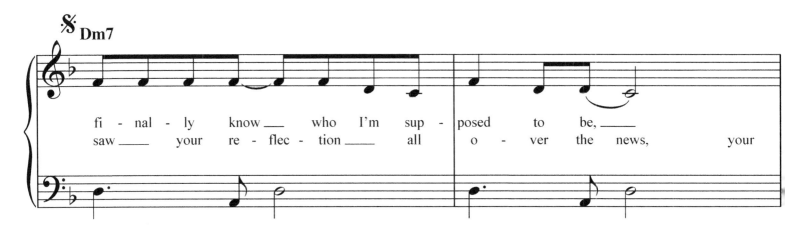

Dm7

fi - nal - ly know ___ who I'm sup - posed to be, ___
saw ___ your re - flec - tion ___ all o - ver the news, your

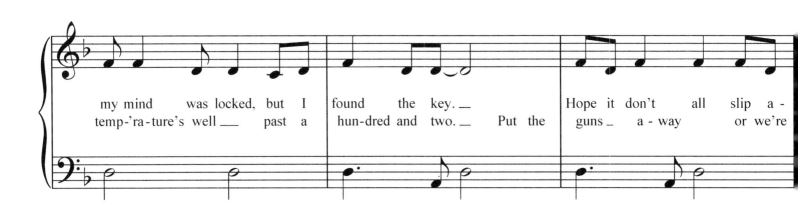

my mind was locked, but I found the key. ___ Hope it don't all slip a-
temp-'ra-ture's well ___ past a hun-dred and two. ___ Put the guns ___ a - way or we're

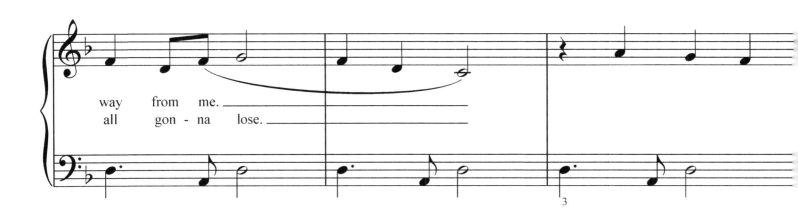

way from me. ___
all gon - na lose. ___

Dm11   D11♭9

Dm11   D11♭9

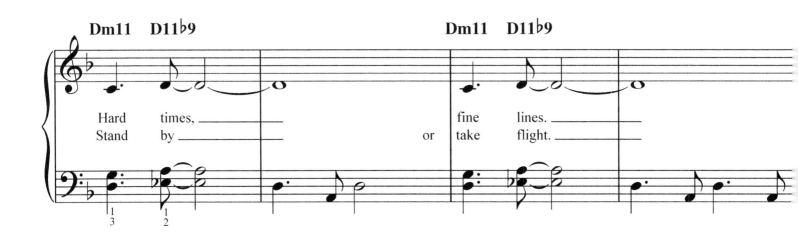

Hard times, ___ fine lines. ___
Stand by ___ or take flight. ___

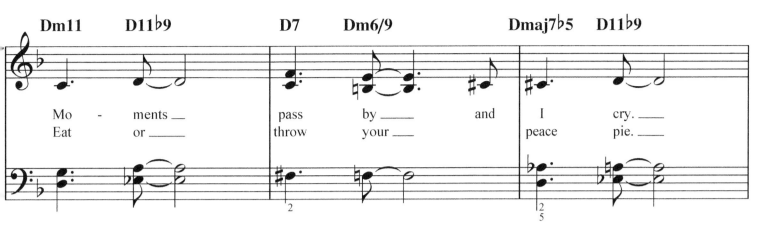

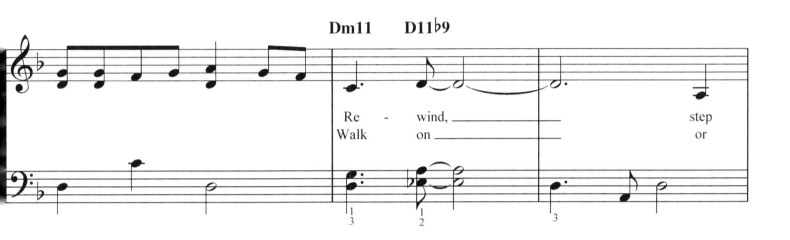

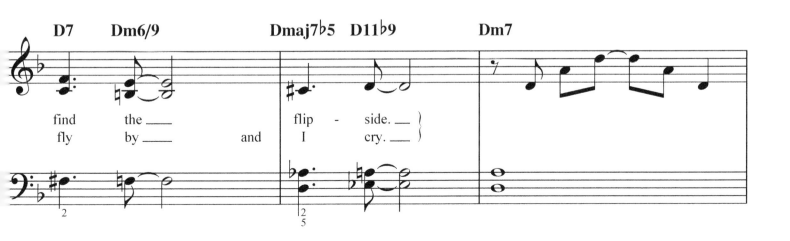

I can't stand

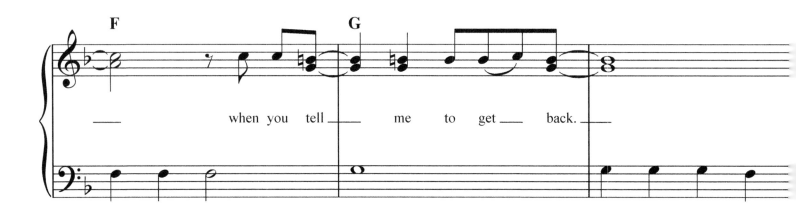

when you tell ___ me to get ___ back. ___

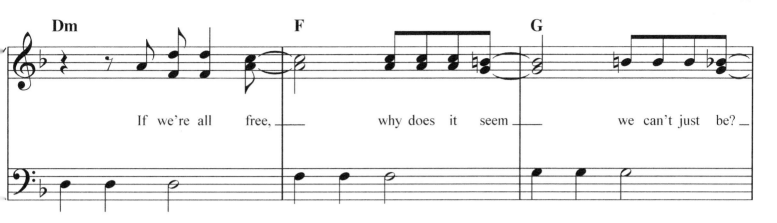

If we're all free, ___ why does it seem ___ we can't just be? ___

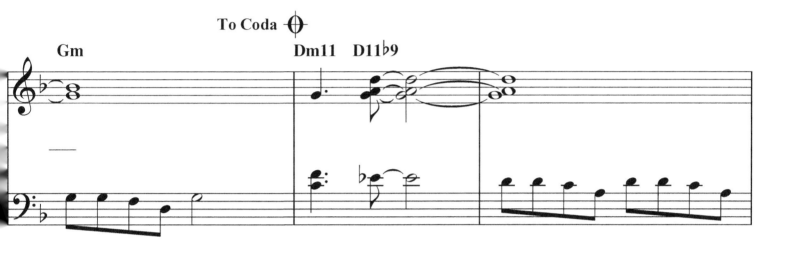

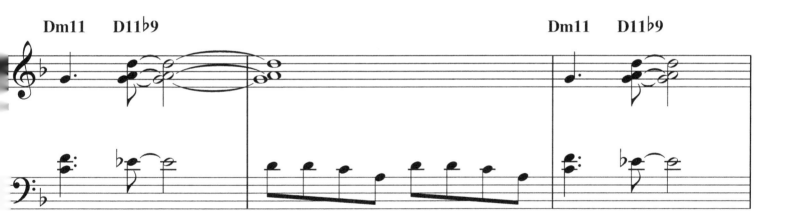

You

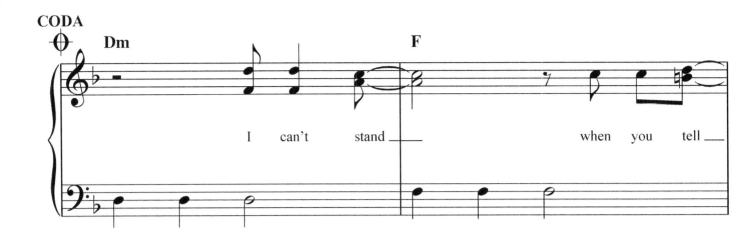

CODA

I can't stand ___ when you tell ___

___ me to get ___ back. ___ If we're all free, ___

___ then why does it seem ___ we can't just be? ___

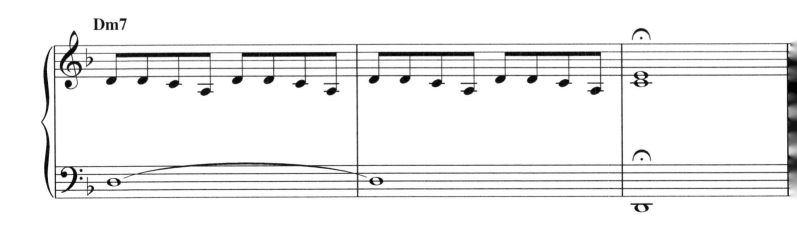

DON'T KNOW WHY

Words and Music by
JESSE HARRIS

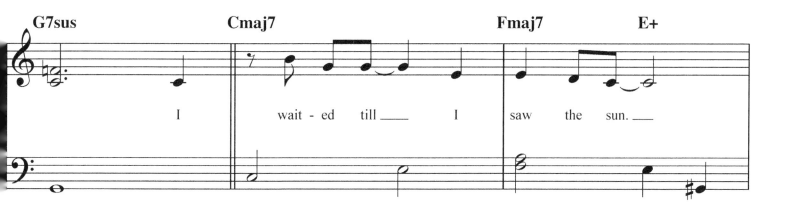

I wait-ed till ___ I saw the sun. ___

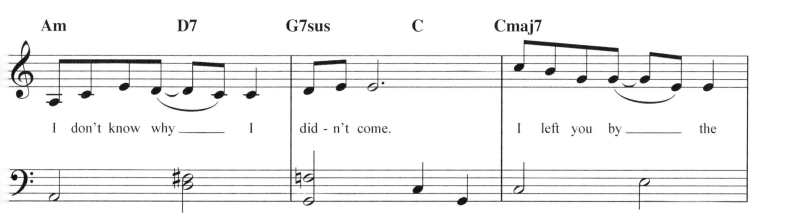

I don't know why ___ I did-n't come. I left you by ___ the

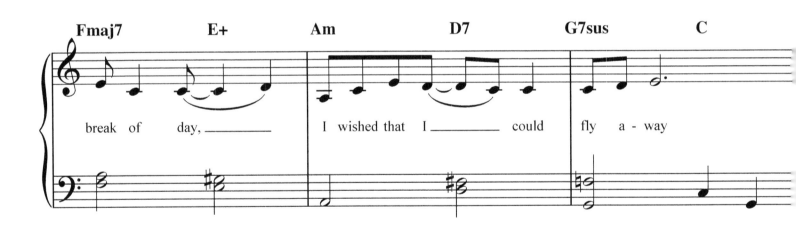

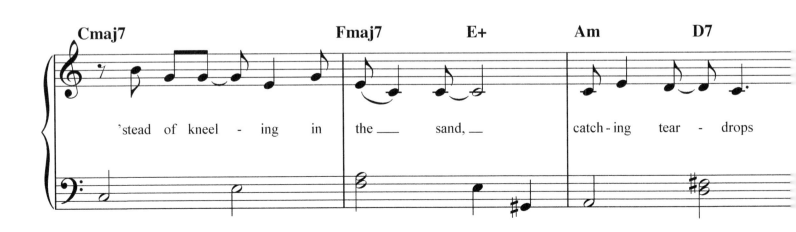

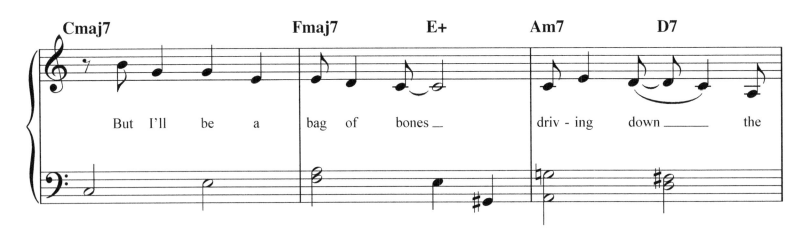

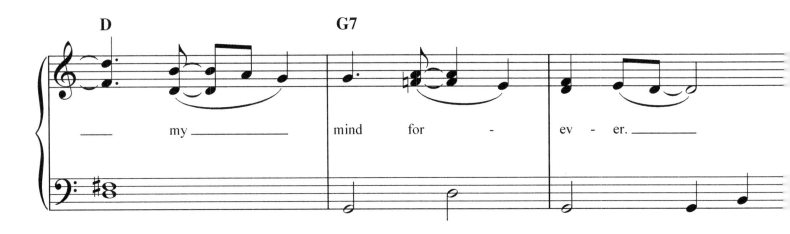

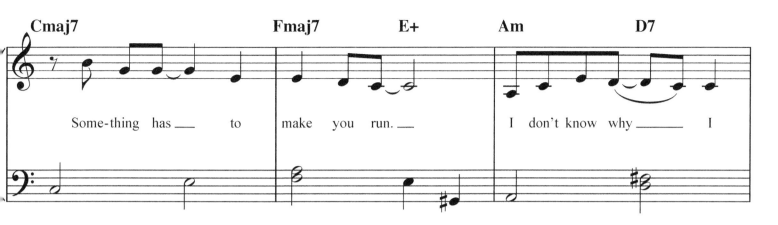

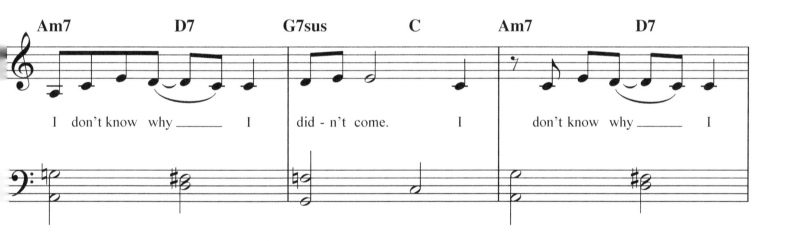

HAPPY PILLS

Words and Music by NORAH JONES
and BRIAN JOSEPH BURTON

Try'n' to pick ___ up the pace; ___ try'n' to make ___ it so I
Nev - er said ___ we'd be friends; ___ try'n' to keep ___ my - self a -

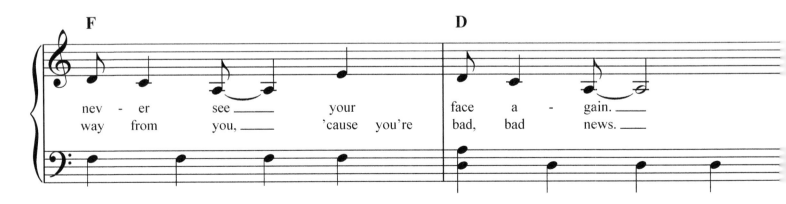

nev - er see ___ your ___ face a - gain. ___
way from you, ___ 'cause you're bad, bad news. ___

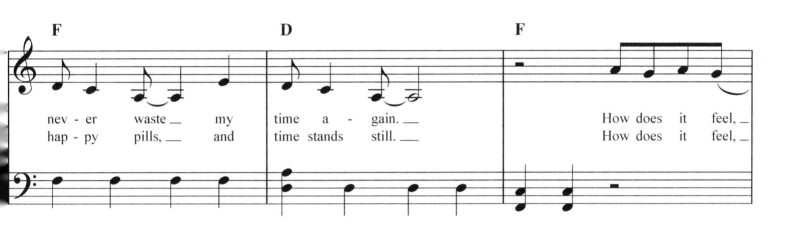

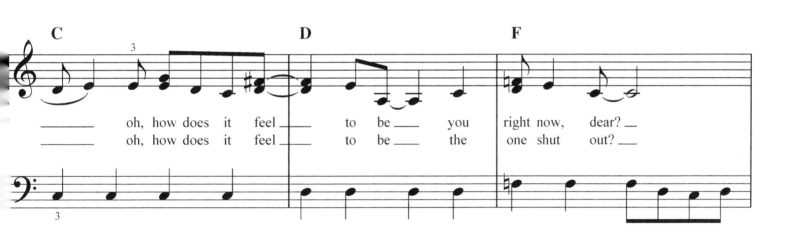

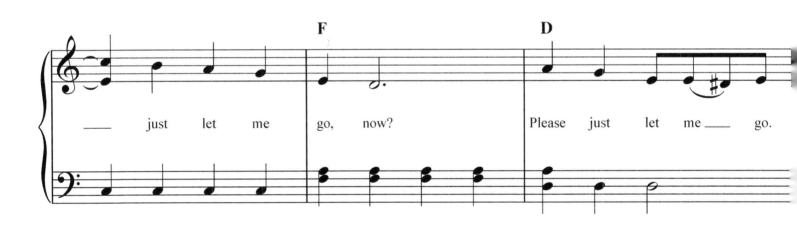

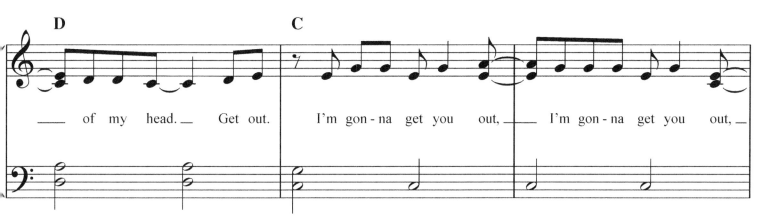

D   **C**

__ of my head. __ Get out.   I'm gon-na get you out, __ I'm gon-na get you out, __

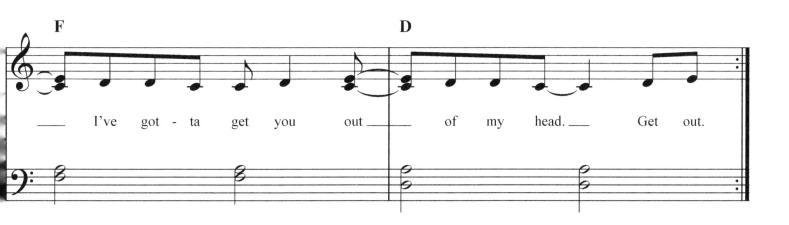

F   **D**

__ I've got-ta get you out __ of my head. __ Get out.

C

I'M ALIVE

Words and Music by NORAH JONES
and JEFF TWEEDY

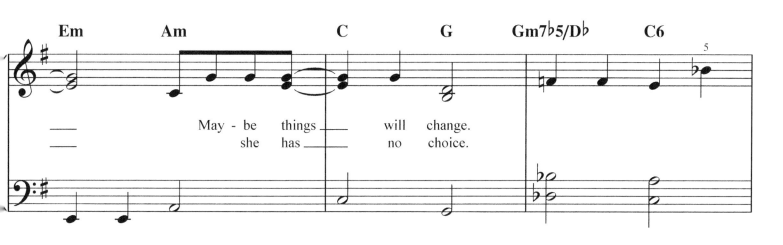

He screams, he __ shouts; _ the

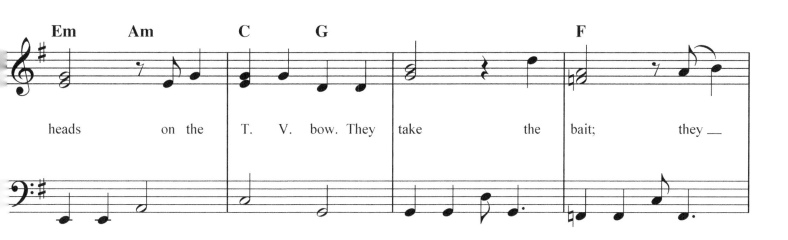

heads on the T. V. bow. They take the bait; they __

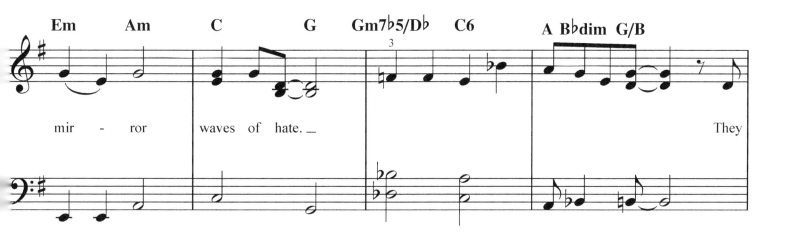

mir - ror waves of hate. _ They

break down walls _____ to free their sins, _____ and

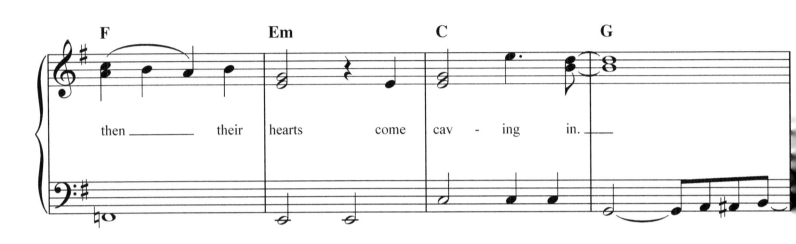

then _____ their hearts come cav - ing in. _____

Oh, I watch, I think, I dance, and some-times _

_____ I drink. I'll sing my songs, I'll hope some-one

35

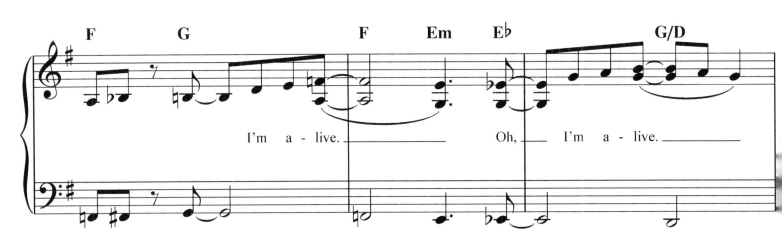

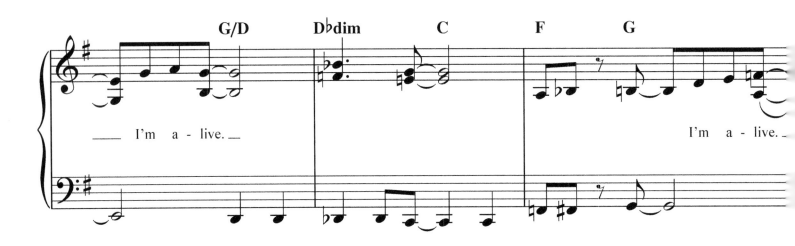

IT WAS YOU

Words and Music by
NORAH JONES

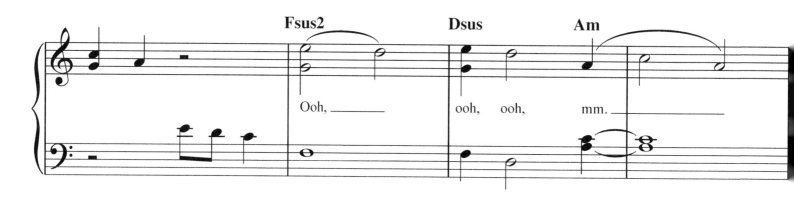

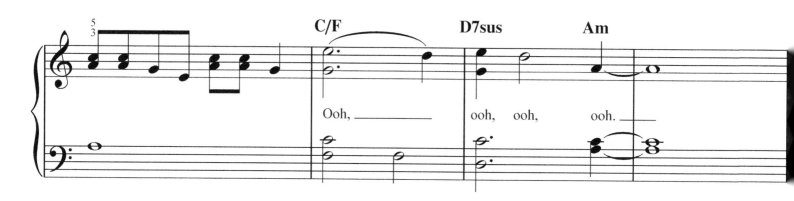

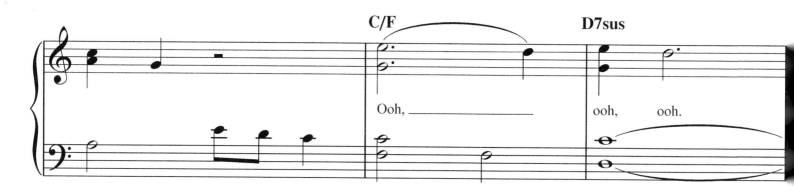

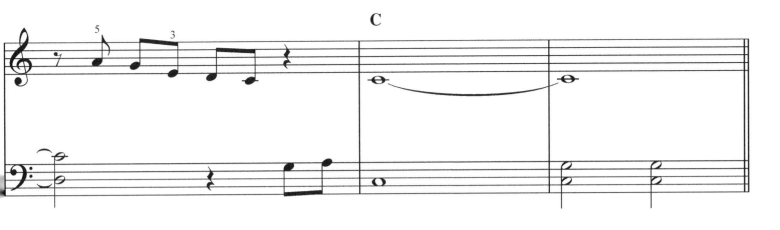

C

En - ter ____ the ____ nights, all ____ re - main. ____
Mo - ments ____ fall ____ like crim - son nights. ____

Make me ____ get ____ up off ____ my feet. ____
Some stick ____ to ____ my skin ____ to - night. ____

Am   C

Take the ____ beat ____
Take a ____ breath ____

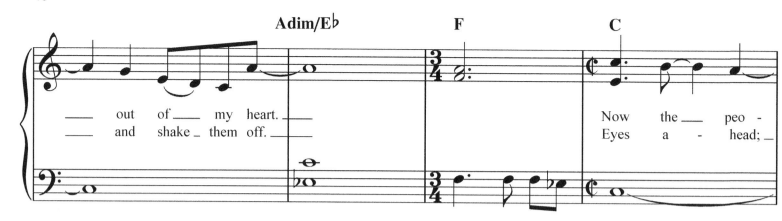

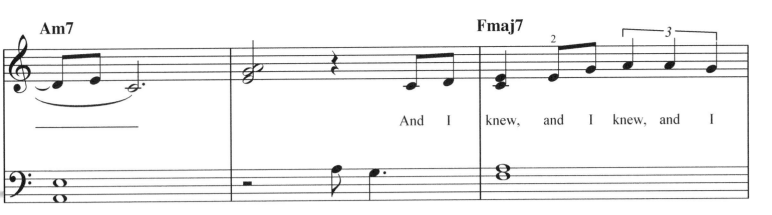

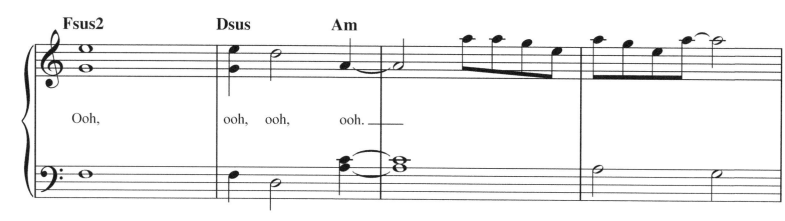

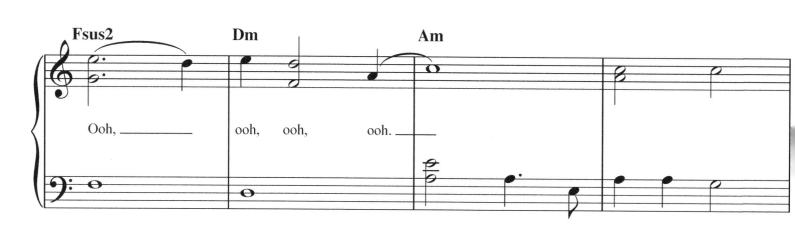

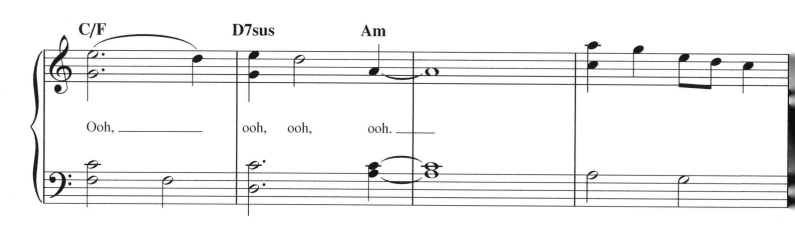

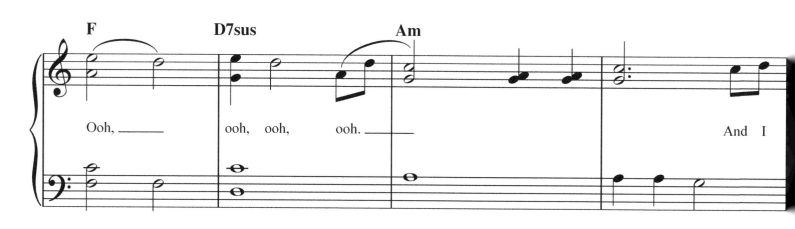

knew, and I knew, and I knew, and I knew it was you. ___ And I

knew, and I knew, and I knew, I knew it was you. _____

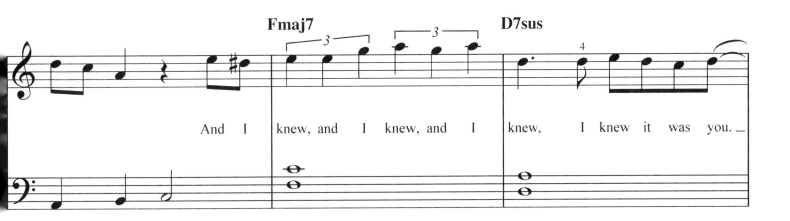

And I knew, and I knew, and I knew, I knew it was you. _

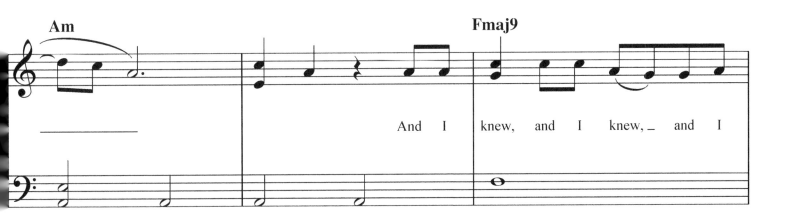

_____ And I knew, and I knew, _ and I

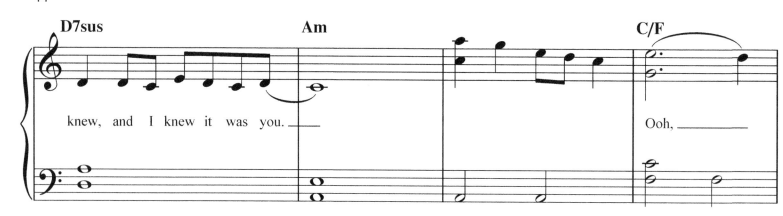

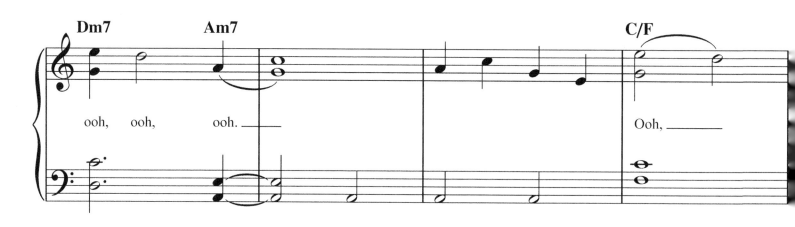

IT'S GONNA BE

Words and Music by
NORAH JONES

If all we talk ___ a-bout is mon-ey, noth-ing will be fun-ny, hon-

-ey. _____

And now that ev - 'ry-one's a crit - ic, it's

mak - ing my mas - ca - ra run - ny. _____

If we on - ly talk _

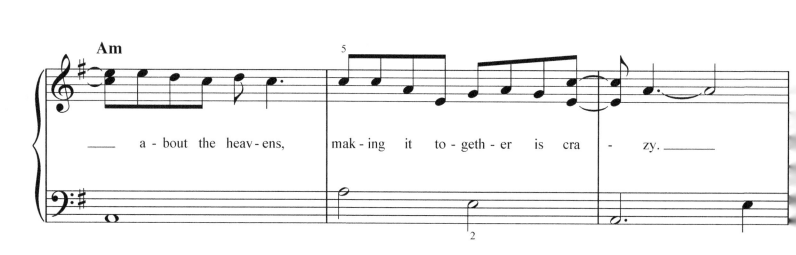

_____ a - bout the heav - ens, mak - ing it to - geth - er is cra - zy. _____

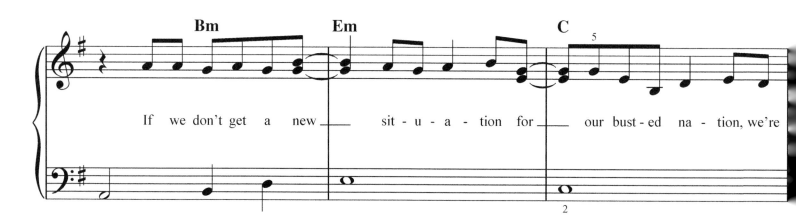

If we don't get a new _____ sit - u - a - tion for _____ our bust - ed na - tion, we're

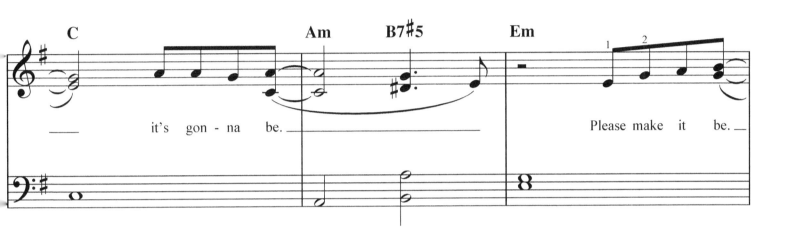

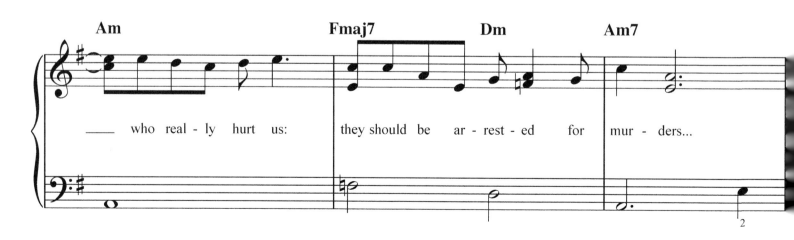

But then all the cam - - 'ras were turned on some skin - ny, na-ked blonde eat-ing bur-

- gers. _____ But it's gon - na be, _____

_____ it's gon - na be, _____ it's gon - na be, _____

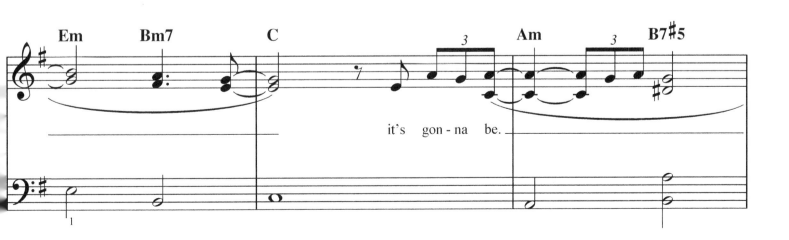

_____ it's gon - na be. _____

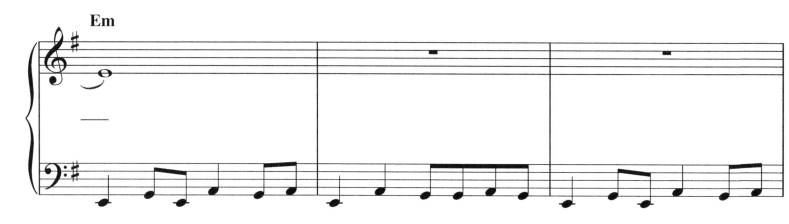

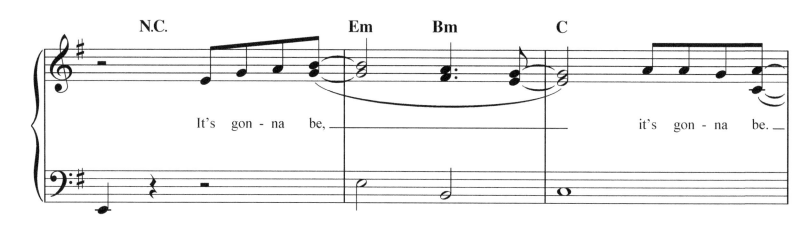

It's gon - na be, _____ it's gon - na be. _

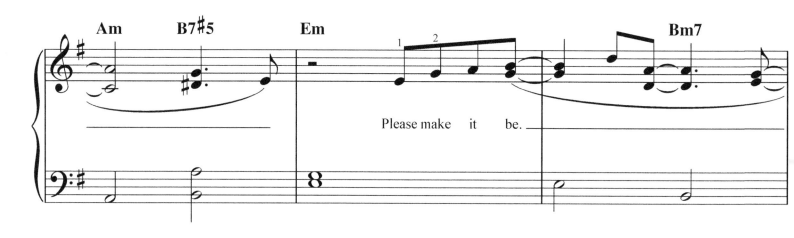

Please make it be. _

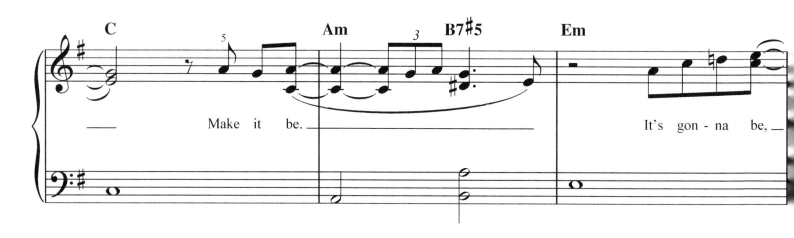

Make it be. _____ It's gon - na be, _

it's gon - na be,

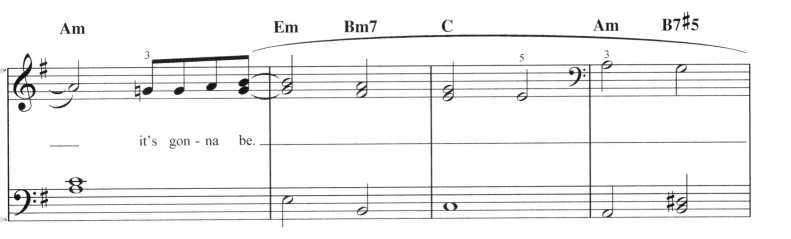

it's gon - na be.

NOT TOO LATE

Words and Music by NORAH JONES
and LEE ALEXANDER

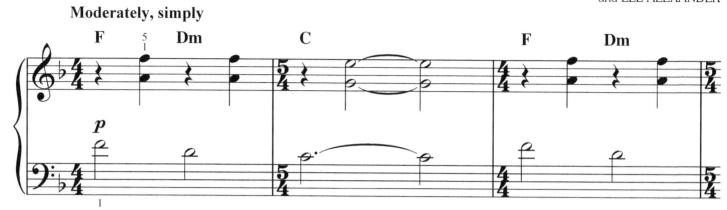

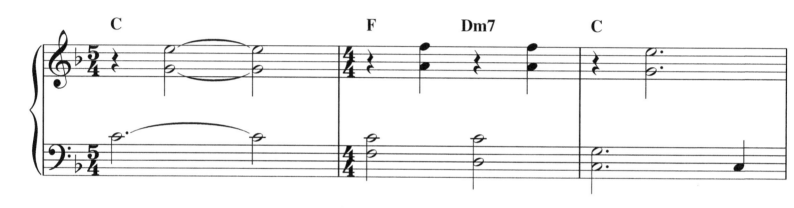

Tell me how you've
My ___ lungs are

been,
out of air,

and tell me what you've seen.
and yours are hold - ing smoke,

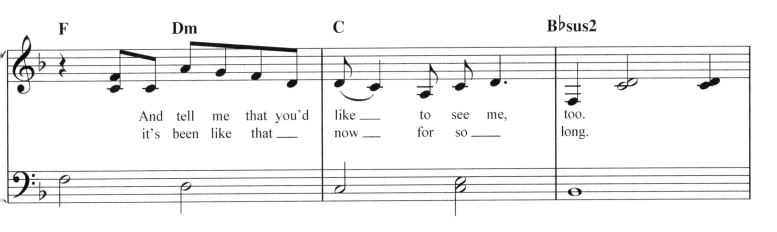

And tell me that you'd like __ to see me, too.
it's been like that __ now __ for so __ long.

'Cause my heart is full __ of no __ blood
And I've seen __ peo - ple try to change,

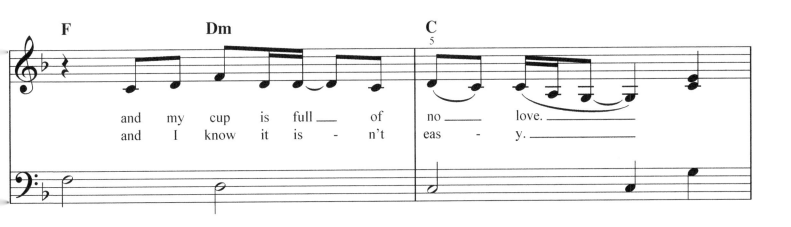

and my cup is full __ of no __ love. __
and I know it is - n't eas - y. __

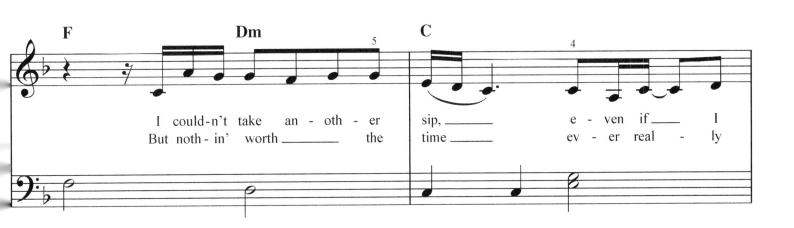

I could-n't take an - oth - er sip, __ e - ven if __ I
But noth - in' worth __ the time __ ev - er real - ly

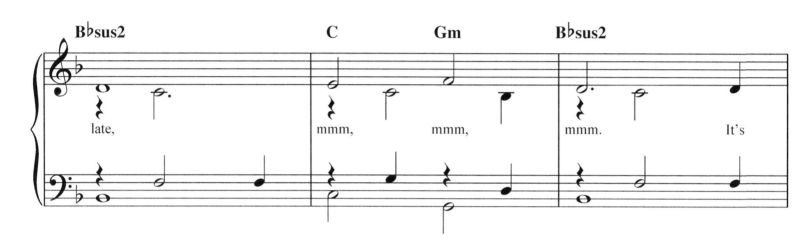

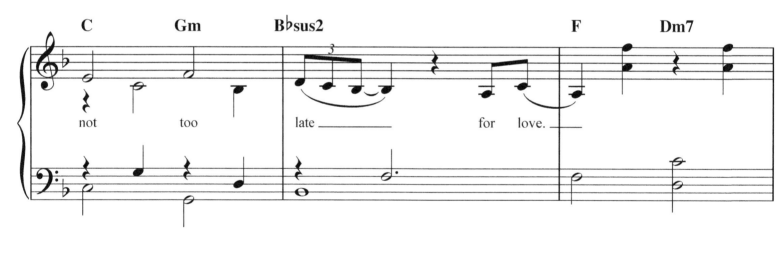

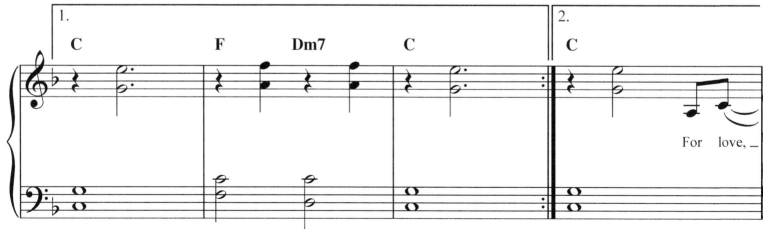

for love, ___

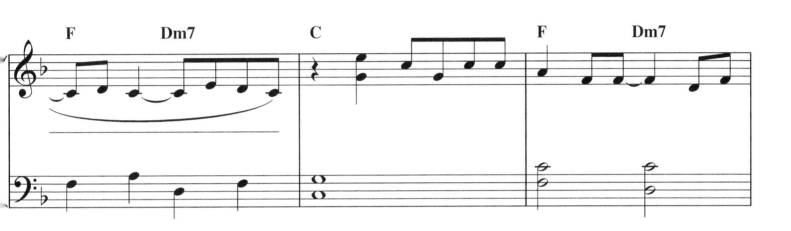

for love. ___

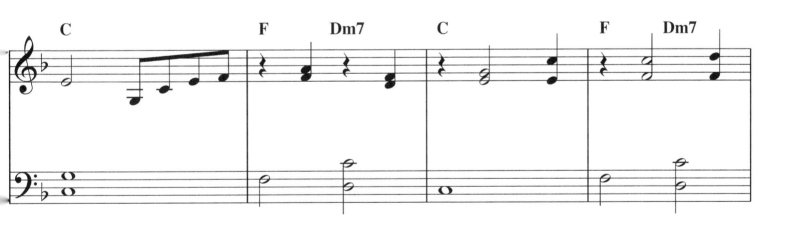

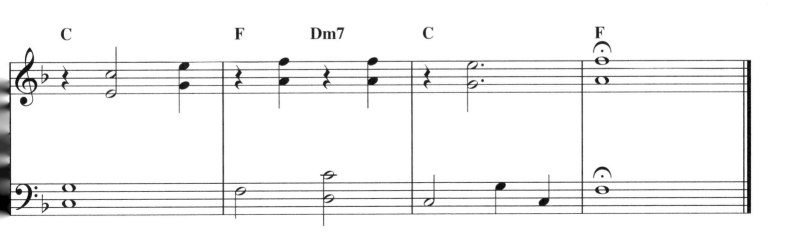

SUNRISE

Words and Music by NORAH JONES
and LEE ALEXANDER

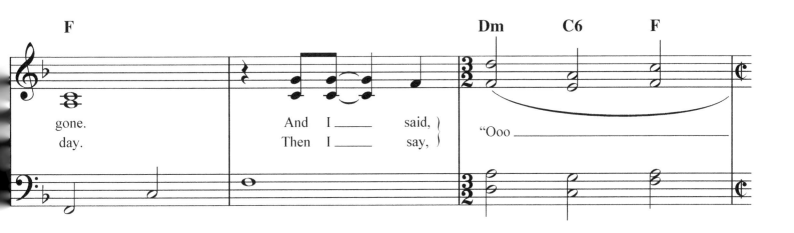

CODA

F   **G/B**

Instrumental ends   And

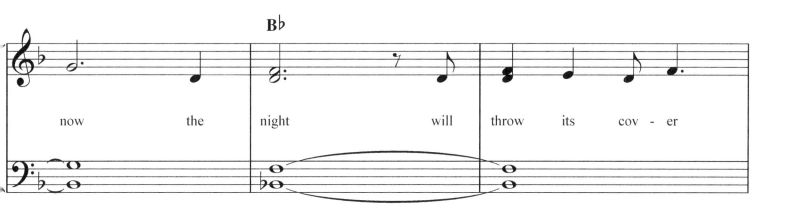

B♭

now   the   night   will   throw   its   cov - er

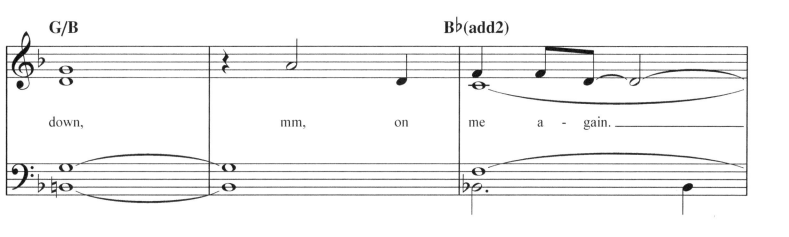

G/B   **B♭(add2)**

down,   mm,   on   me   a - gain. _____

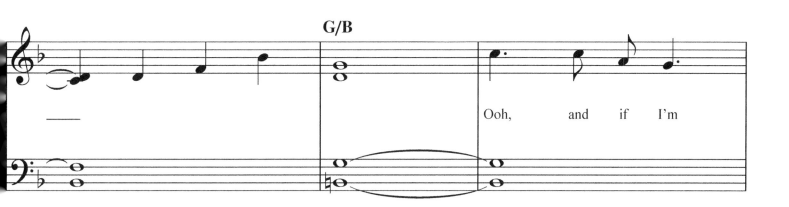

G/B

_____   Ooh,   and   if   I'm

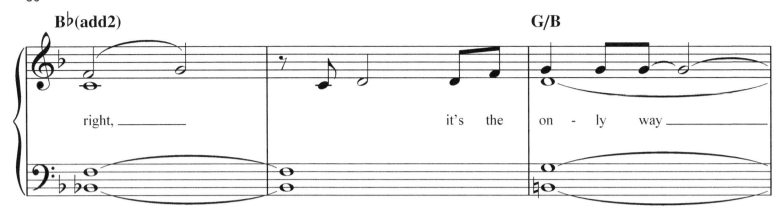

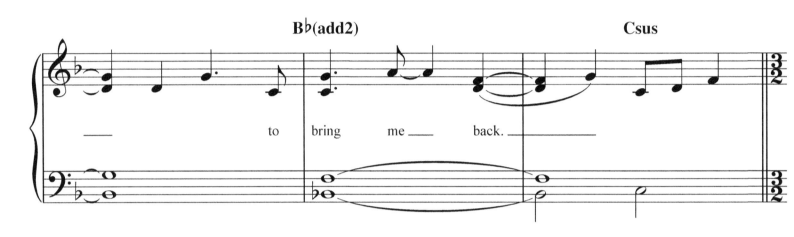

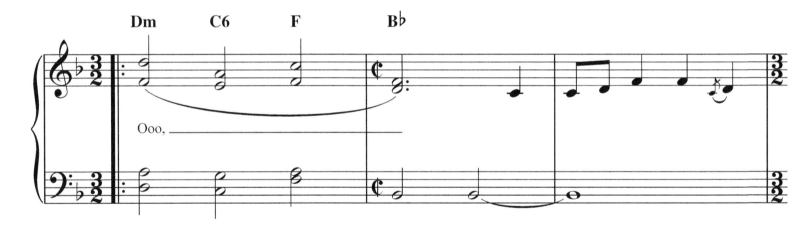

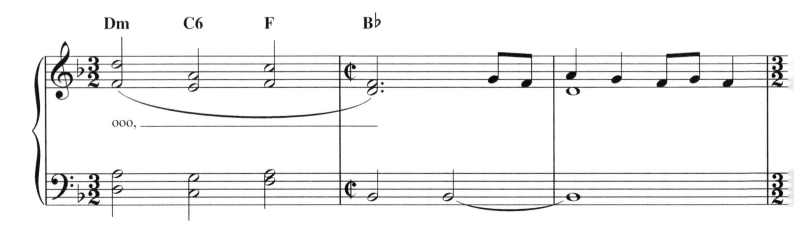

THINKING ABOUT YOU

Words and Music by NORAH JONES
and ILHAN ERSAHIN

Slowly, in 2

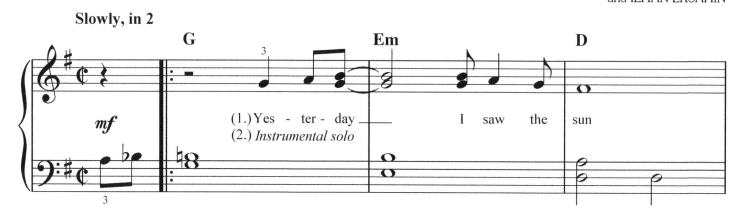

(1.) Yes - ter - day _____ I saw the sun

(2.) *Instrumental solo*

shin - ing, and the leaves _____ were fall - ing down _____

soft - ly. And my cold hands _____ need-ed a warm, warm _____

touch, _____ and I was think - ing a - bout _____ you.

But here I am, ____
Solo ends So when you sail ____

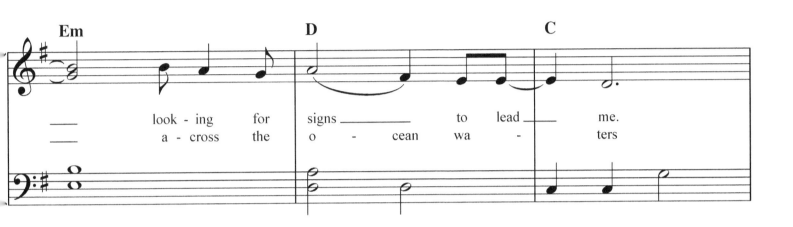

____ look - ing for signs ____ to lead ____ me.
____ a - cross the o - cean wa - ters

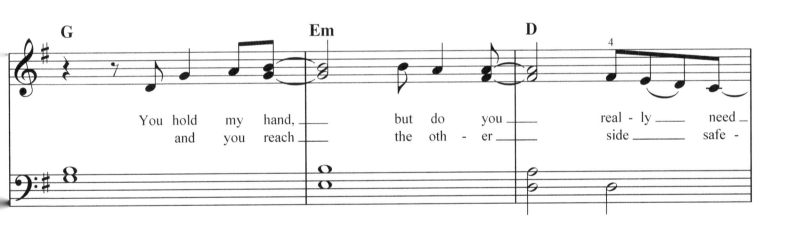

You hold my hand, ____ but do you ____ real - ly ____ need ____
and you reach ____ the oth - er ____ side ____ safe -

____ me?
- ly,
I guess it's time ____ for me to
could you smile ____ a lit - tle

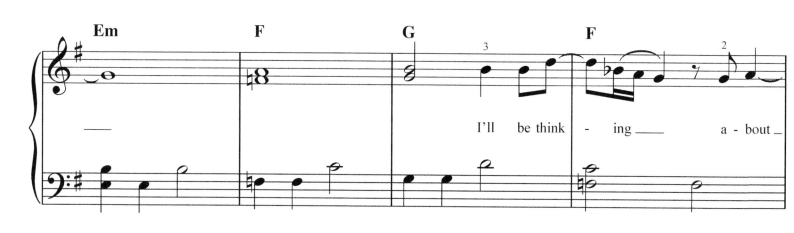

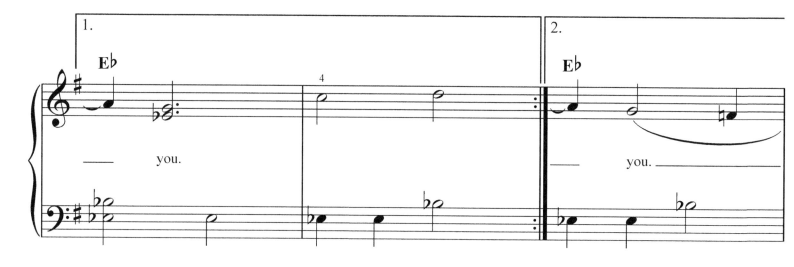

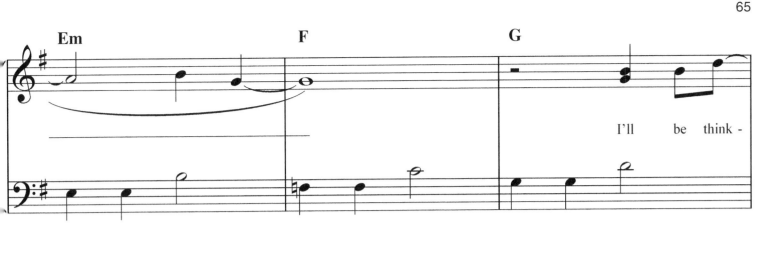

I'll be think-

-ing a - bout you.

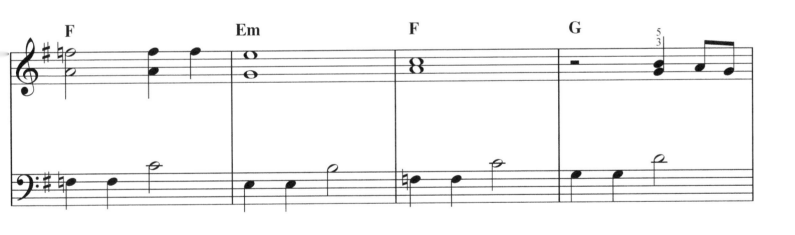

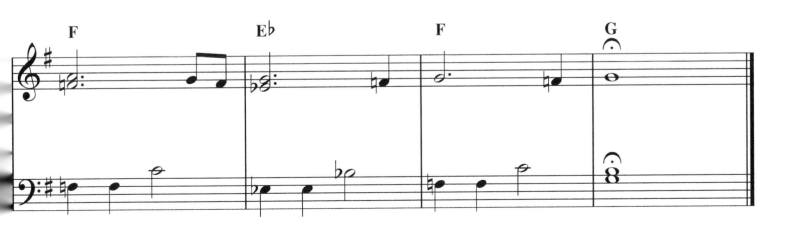

WHAT AM I TO YOU

Words and Music by
NORAH JONES

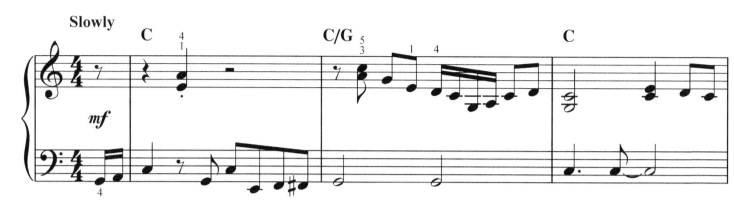

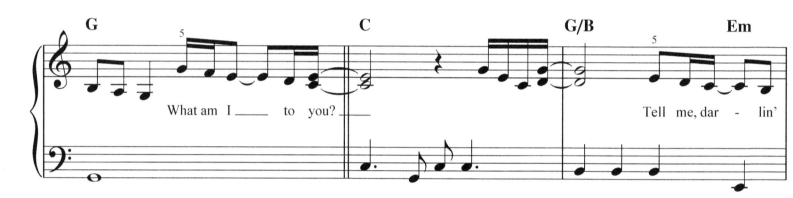

What am I _____ to you? _____ Tell me, dar - lin'

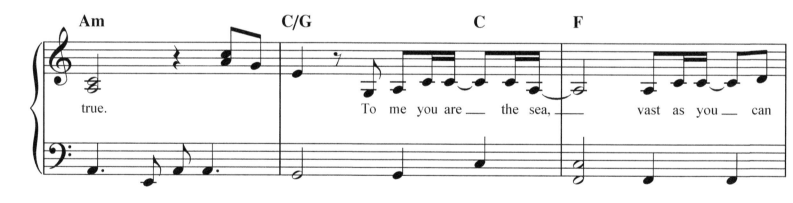

true. To me you are _____ the sea, _____ vast as you _____ can

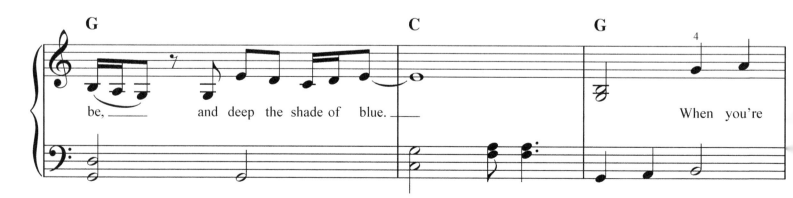

be, _____ and deep the shade of blue. _____ When you're

feel - in' low, _____ oh, to whom else do ____ you go?
(Instrumental solo on D.S.)

See, I'd cry if you hurt; I'd give you my ___ last shirt be - cause I love you

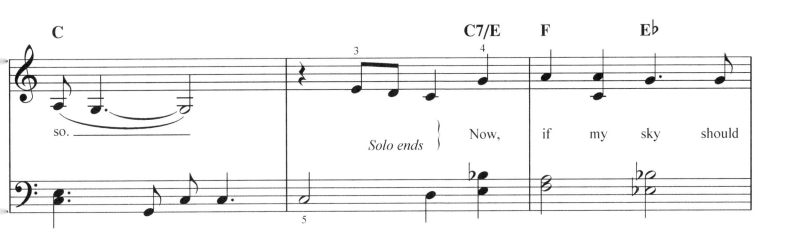

so. _____ *Solo ends* Now, if my sky should

fall, would you e - ven call? ___ I've o-pened up ___ my
I'll o - pen up ___ my

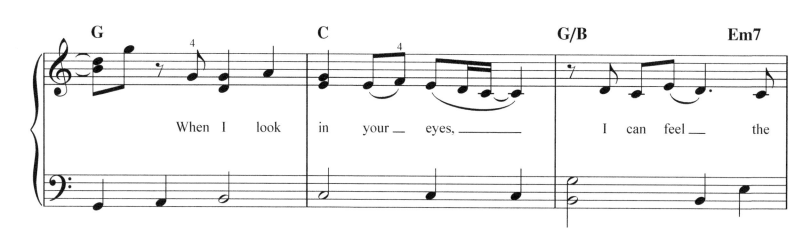

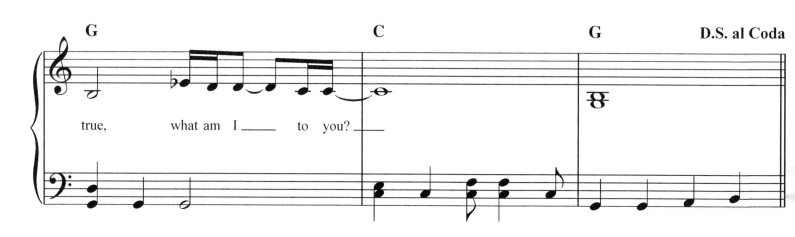

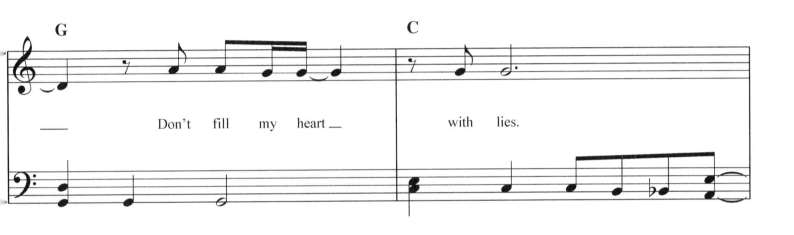

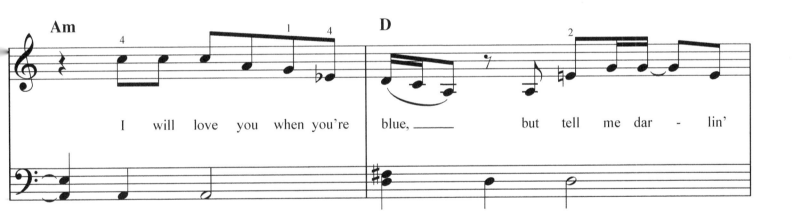

SAY GOODBYE

Words and Music by NORAH JONES
and BRIAN JOSEPH BURTON

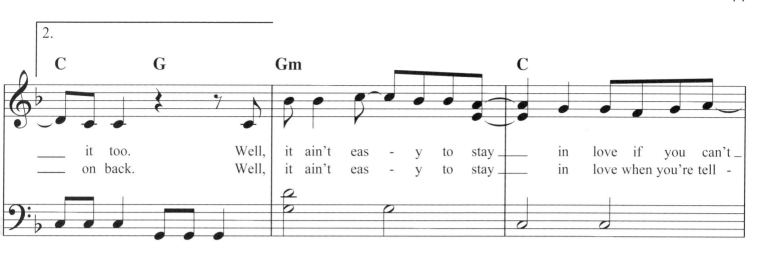

it too. Well, it ain't eas - y to stay ___ in love if you can't _

on back. Well, it ain't eas - y to stay ___ in love when you're tell -

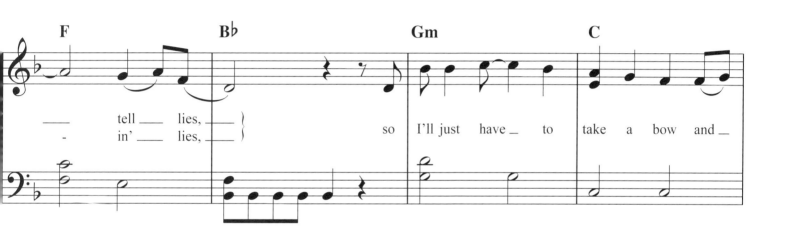

tell ___ lies, ___ so I'll just have _ to take a bow and _

- in' ___ lies, ___

say good - bye. ___ Ooh. _

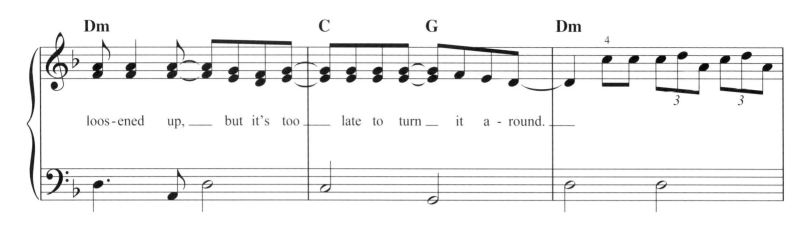

loos-ened up, ___ but it's too ___ late to turn ___ it a - round. ___

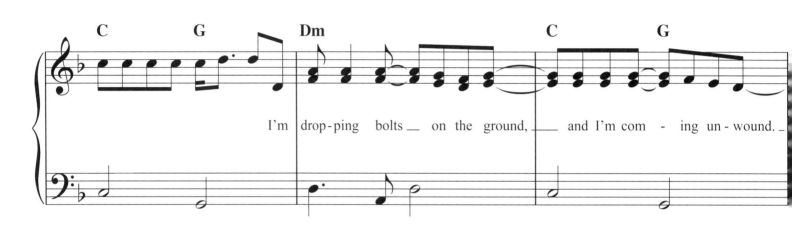

I'm drop-ping bolts ___ on the ground, ___ and I'm com - ing un - wound. ___

D.S. al Coda
(take 2nd ending)

CODA

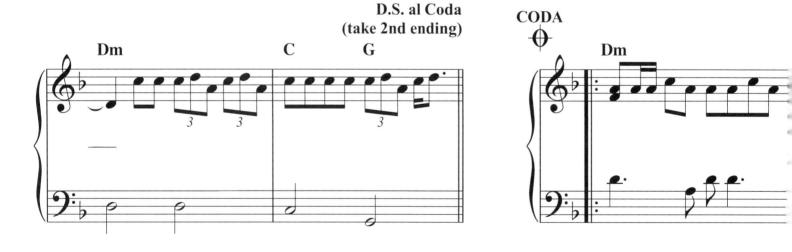

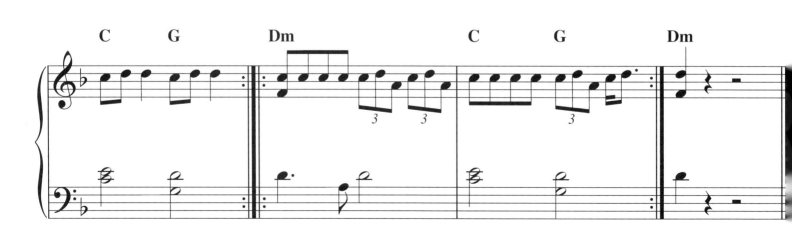